The Thrill of the Ride

Laura Purdie Salas

STECK-VAUGHN
ELEMENTARY · SECONDARY · ADULT · LIBRARY

A Harcourt Company

www.steck-vaughn.com

Many thanks to "Terrible" Terry McChesney for his review of this book.

Photography: Cover ©Duomo/CORBIS; p.iii ©Phil Schermeister/CORBIS; p.iv ©Bettmann/CORBIS; p.3 ©Steve Wilkings; p.4 ©Ales Fevzer/CORBIS; p.8 ©Richard Hamilton Smith/CORBIS; p.10 ©David Young-Wolff/PhotoEdit; p.15 ©Eric Pearle/FPG; p.18 ©Adam Pretty/AllSport; p.19 ©Duomo/CORBIS; p.21 ©Duomo/CORBIS; p.22 ©Duomo/CORBIS; p.23 ©Mike Powell/AllSport.

Additional photography by Comstock and PhotoDisc.

Contents

Early skateboards were flat, and riders didn't have safety gear.

Chapter 1

The Story of Skateboarding

Skateboarding has had a bumpy ride for more than 70 years. Sometimes it has been more popular than at other times, but skateboarding has never **disappeared**. Now, skateboarding is popular again. It seems that it may be here to stay. What makes so many people love this sport? To find out, check out the story of skateboarding.

The Ride Begins

Skateboards were first used in the 1930s. **Skaters** joined boards to **metal** roller-skate wheels. The hard metal wheels of the skateboards would bang along sidewalks.

Kids couldn't get better wheels. They didn't have other **choices**. Stores didn't sell skateboards until about 25 years after the skateboard was invented.

Skateboards at the Store

In 1958, toy makers began to design and make skateboards. The first skateboards sold in stores were made of wood. A few were made from **plastic**. Wooden boards were heavy and didn't bend very much. Plastic boards bent too much.

Soon toy makers began using clay wheels on skateboards. Clay wheels didn't make as much noise as metal wheels.

Skating Becomes Popular

In the early 1960s, skateboarding became very popular. **Surfers** were interested in skateboarding. Surfers rode waves like skaters rode on land. They listened to songs such as "Surfin' U.S.A." by the Beach Boys. There was

Riding a surfboard is like riding a skateboard on water.

one problem. Surfers could only surf at the beach during good weather.

Surfers began skating. They called it sidewalk surfing. A new song came out by Jan and Dean called "Sidewalk Surfing." Thanks to the surfers, skating was bigger than ever.

Skating Comes and Goes

In 1965, everyone saw the first National Skateboard Championship on TV.

A **magazine** ran a story on the thrills and dangers of skating. Doctors also pointed out the dangers of skating. Suddenly everyone was talking about skateboarding. By the end of 1965, skating didn't seem so cool anymore. Many skaters stopped skating.

In 1971, Richard Stevenson designed a board that **curved** up at the back. This tail made the board easier to move. In 1973, surfer Frank Nasworthy found a better wheel for skateboards. The wheel was made of a new kind of plastic. The wheel was strong, but softer than clay. Frank tried out the new wheels. They made his ride smoother and quieter. The wheels were named Cadillacs because they rode as smoothly as Cadillac cars.

Skateboard wheels come in many colors.

In a few years, skating had made another **comeback**. Kids skated in empty swimming pools and city streets. Skaters also rode in new skate parks. Some kids still rode on wooden boards. Others used new boards that were made from wood and plastic. These boards were strong and could slide really well.

More Ups and Downs

In the early 1980s, skating was on its way out again. City governments had passed skating **laws**. These laws said that skaters couldn't skate on sidewalks or streets. The country of Norway didn't let anyone skate at all! The laws were passed because people were worried that skaters could get hurt.

Skating wasn't gone for very long. In the late 1980s, it was back again. Skateboarders built ramps and skated in their backyards. New skateboards had curved ends that made the boards stronger and easier to move.

Skaters started dressing in a certain way. They wore big T-shirts and long shorts. Lots of kids listened to music while they skated. For many, skating had become a way of life.

Skaters Everywhere

In the 1990s, skating became more popular all over the world. The ESPN X Games started in 1995. Skaters from many countries skated for money and prizes. Most skaters still used boards made of wood and plastic. These boards were light and springy.

More Challenging Choices

Today's skaters have more choices than skaters did in the past. Boards are stronger and give a smoother ride. Great new tricks are being invented. Skating today is also more challenging than it was in the past. Finding safe places to skate is difficult. To many skaters, though, the thrill of skating is worth the work.

Chapter 2

Where Skaters Can Skate

Today, many cities only allow skating in certain places. Some laws say that skaters can't skate on sidewalks or streets. Other laws do not allow skaters to ride in city parks.

Skaters need to learn their cities' laws. Then they will know what choices and rights they have.

Street Skating

Street skaters skate on streets, sidewalks, and other **objects**. Many skaters jump on and off curbs. They may even skate along park benches.

Street skaters can't skate any way that they want. Skaters must follow their cities' laws.

Most laws say skaters must face the same **direction** as cars and other vehicles. Skaters must also obey street signs. ⚡

Skate Parks

Some skaters may not like all the rules of street skating. These skaters might choose to skate at a skate park. Skate parks allow skaters more **freedom**. There are no cars or people in the way. Skaters are free to practice their moves.

Skate parks offer lots of fun for skaters.

Skate parks have lots of great features, such as ramps, bumps, and half pipes. A half pipe is a U-shaped ramp with a flat part in the middle.

Skate parks are very popular with skaters, but skate parks had a difficult start. The first big skate park was built in Florida in 1976. Many park **owners** could not pay for insurance. **Insurance** would help owners pay people who got hurt in skating parks. By 1980, most park owners had closed their parks.

Skate parks made a comeback in the late 1990s. Insurance doesn't cost as much. Now owners can pay for it and keep their parks open. Today, most skate parks are run by cities. In 2001, there were more than 1,000 skate parks in the United States. Today's skate parks still have bumps, ramps, and half pipes. They also have street objects, such as benches and curbs.

Making Good Choices

Choosing the best spot to skate can be challenging. Some skaters like street skating. Other skaters like skate parks. No matter where they skate, skaters need to make good choices. If skaters break laws, city governments might pass more laws. Then skaters might have even fewer places to skate.

Skaters need to make good choices about where to skate.

Chapter 3

The Board and Its Parts

If you have found a place to skate, you've done the hard part. Learning to skate is fairly easy. First, take a look at a skateboard. It's important to learn how its parts work.

Parts of a Skateboard

Skateboards have three main parts. They are the deck, the trucks, and the wheels.

The deck is the part you stand on. It is also called the board. The deck is curved in front and back. Skaters press their feet against these parts of the deck during many tricks.

Two trucks join the wheels to the deck. Trucks let you **steer** your board in any direction. You can move left or right. You can go straight ahead or move **backward**.

deck

truck   wheel

11

Skateboard wheels come in different sizes. Big wheels make the board go fast. Small wheels are better for tricks.

Kinds of Skateboards

Now that you know what the parts do, it's time to choose your board. There are two kinds of boards, plain boards and long boards.

If you're a beginning skater, buy a plain board designed for street and park skating. Try to buy a **stiff** board that doesn't bend. It's easier to stand on and won't rock too much.

If you're an **advanced** skater, you have more choices. You can buy parts, then put the parts together to build a **custom** board. If you like doing tricks, look for special parts. Choose a smaller, lighter deck that will pop up easily. Look for small, hard wheels that will make sharper turns.

If you want to skate on hills and streets, pick a long board. You might also choose

Choose a long board to skate on hills and streets.

large, soft wheels to make your ride smooth and fast.

Whatever board you choose, there's one thing you must not skate without. It doesn't matter if you're a beginning or an advanced skater. You've got to wear safety **gear**.

Chapter 4

Put on Your Gear and Go!

More than thirty thousand skaters go to the hospital every year. Many skaters hurt their **wrists** from holding their hands out to break a fall. Many also hurt their heads. Other **injuries** are broken bones and cuts.

Skating has a high number of injuries. That's why it's so important that you wear the right gear. Safety gear **protects** your body if you fall or run into something.

What to Wear

A beginning skater just needs a few pieces of safety gear. Most important is a helmet to protect your head. **Elbow pads** and knee pads protect your arms and legs. Wrist **guards** keep

your wrists from bending the wrong way
or breaking.

Getting Started

You've found a place to skate, and you have
your gear. It's time to get on the board. Place
your feet **sideways** with one foot at each end
of the board. Bend your knees a bit. Now get
ready to learn some moves.

Put your feet on the board and bend your knees a bit.

The first move to learn is gliding. Put one foot in the middle of the deck. Your foot should be facing **forward**. Then push off with your other foot. Practice gliding on one foot first.

The second move is carving. This is skating in a big half circle. Lean forward while gliding. The board will go the same direction you are leaning. Lean back to make the board go the other way.

The third move is jumping off your board. This is also called bailing. You should bail if you are going too fast or if you are about to crash. After you bail, run a few steps on the ground. This should keep you from falling down.

It will take a while to learn these three skating moves. Once you've learned them, you might want to try some tricks. Maybe you'll get so good at skating, you'll win a **contest**!

Chapter 5

Skating Tricks and Contests

Skating tricks have come a long way since the 1960s. Now skaters do jumps, spins, and flips that look **impossible**. Skaters are inventing new tricks all the time.

Amazing Tricks

Almost every skater learns two tricks. These tricks are the wheelie and the ollie. In a wheelie, the two front wheels come off the ground. For an ollie, the skater kicks the board's tail onto the ground. As the front of the board rises, the skater jumps. The board follows the skater off the ground.

Some skateboard tricks take the rider up in the air.

Another trick is a 50-50 grind. For this trick, the skater grinds the trucks along a railing or curb. Only the insides of the wheels touch the object.

Advanced skaters do harder tricks. One trick is the frontside 180 ollie. This is a special kind of ollie. The skater jumps into the air and spins around with the board. Both skater and

New skateboard tricks are being invented all the time.

board land facing the other direction. They
skate away in the same direction they were
going.

The 540 shove-it is even more difficult than
the frontside 180. For the 540, a skater jumps
up off the board while the board turns in the
air one and **one-half** times. Then the skater
lands on the board and glides forward.

New skaters might think they'll never learn the coolest tricks. But the best skaters were once beginning skaters, too. Watching them is a great way to learn some of the best skateboarding tricks. ⚡

The Best of the Best

Advanced skaters have changed the sport of skating. Some skaters have invented new tricks. Others are just great skaters. Some advanced skaters even become **professionals,** or pros. Pros can make money selling gear with their name on it. They also can make money by skating in contests.

In the 1970s, 13-year-old Alan Gelfand invented the ollie. One day, he used his back foot to pop his board into the air. This trick was named the ollie because Alan's friends called him Ollie.

Tony Hawk is another **famous** skater. Tony turned pro at age 14. He bought his own

Tony Hawk has invented many skating tricks.

house when he was 18! Tony has invented more than 50 skating tricks. In 1999, he was the first to do a 900 at the X Games. A 900 is two and one-half turns in the air on a board.

Another pro skater is Vanessa Torres. At age 14, she won the street part of the 2001 All-Girl Skate Jam. She also won for best trick.

Tony Hawk shows one of his tricks at the X Games.

Contests

There are many popular skating contests all over the world. Contests are for skating tricks or street skating. Some contests are only for **amateur** skaters. Amateur skaters see skating as a **hobby**. They enter contests because they love doing challenging tricks. The pros love skateboarding, too. But they win money for their moves and tricks!

Skating for One and All

Today there are more than six million skaters in America. Most of them are kids, but skaters are many different ages. A teacher could be a skateboarder. So could the man at the fast-food window. A baby just learning to walk could be a skateboarder ten years from now.

All beginning skaters have the same **possibilities**. Any skater could invent the next big trick. That skater might even be you! ⚡

This skater has used his board a lot. It shows on his board and in the tricks he can do.

Glossary

advanced (ad VANST) *adjective* Advanced means very good at something.

amateur (AM uh chuhr) *adjective* Amateur skaters are people who skate for fun, not for money.

backward (bak WUHRD) *adverb* Backward means toward the back.

choices (CHOYS uhz) *noun* Choices are things that you choose between.

comeback (KUHM bak) *noun* A comeback happens when a person or thing that used to be popular becomes popular again.

contest (KAHN tehst) *noun* A contest is a game in which two or more people play against each other. They may play to win money or prizes.

curved (KURVD) *verb* Curved means rounded or bent like part of a circle.

custom (KUHS tuhm) *adjective* Custom means made or done a special way for someone.

direction (duh REHK shuhn) *noun* A direction is the way a person or thing moves. Left, west, and down are all directions.

disappeared (dihs uh PIHRD) *verb* Disappeared means went out of sight.

elbow pads (EHL boh padz) *noun* Elbow pads are wraps that keep the bend of the arm from getting hurt.

famous (FAY muhs) *adjective* Famous means known by many people.

forward (FAWR wuhrd) *adverb* Forward means toward the front.

freedom (FREE duhm) *noun* Freedom is being free to go where you want or to do or say what you want.

gear (GIHR) *noun* Gear is special clothes or other things that you need to do a certain sport.

guards (GAHRDZ) *noun* Guards are things to wear on your arms, legs, or other body parts when playing sports. Guards help keep your body from getting hurt.

hobby (HAHB ee) *noun* A hobby is a thing that you do in your free time, such as skating or building model ships.

impossible (ihm PAHS uh buhl) *adjective* Impossible means cannot be done.

injuries (IHN jhuh reez) *noun* Injuries are hurt places on your body.

insurance (ihn SHUR uhns) *noun* With insurance, an owner pays money to a company. The company agrees to pay the owner for losses from fires or accidents. Insurance may also pay for people who get badly hurt at a place that belongs to the owner.

laws (LAWZ) *noun* Laws are rules made by a city, state, or country. Laws tell you what you can and cannot do.

magazine (MAG uh zeen) *noun* A magazine is a paper booklet that has stories and pictures in it.

metal (MEHT uhl) *adjective* Metal means made of iron or another shiny solid, such as silver.

objects (AHB jehkts) *noun* Objects are things that can be seen or touched.

one-half (wuhn HAF) *adjective* One-half is one of two parts of a whole. It is the same size as the other part.

owners (OH nuhrs) *noun* Owners are people that stores, skate parks, or other places belong to.

plastic (PLAS tihk) *noun* Plastic is a solid used to make strong objects.

possibilities (pahs uh BIHL uh teez) *noun* Possibilities are all the different things that could happen.

professionals (proh FEHSH uh nuhlz) *noun* Professionals are people who become very good at something and make money doing it. Pro is short for professional.

protects (proh TEHKTS) *verb* Protects means keeps something or someone from getting hurt.

sideways (SYD wayz) *adverb* Sideways means toward the side.

skaters (SKAYT uhrz) *noun* Skaters are people who ride skateboards.

steer (STIHR) *verb* To steer means to move something the way you want it to go.

stiff (STIHF) *adjective* Stiff means hard and not bending.

surfers (SURF uhrs) *noun* Surfers are people who ride ocean waves on surfboards.

wrists (RIHSTS) *noun* Wrists are the body parts that join your hands to your arms.

Index